Motivating Feedback:
Getting The Most From Your Employees Without Tears

Laurie Leiker

DEDICATION

For Sarah

CONTENTS

ACKNOWLEDGMENTS

Many thanks go to more people than I could possibly mention, as everyone who has touched my life has helped me get to this point. I definitely need to thank Suzie Kummins-Poirer and Patti Blackstaffe for being the best business support system a person can have. Thanks go to the Central Austin Jelly crew, including Ilene Haddad, Tom Myer, Hope Doty and Ansa Copeland. Amanda Quraishi for all her love and support, even when I didn't deserve it. To my very large and extended family – much love.

Image credit: <u>123RF Stock Photos</u>

 1 WHAT IS FEEDBACK?

LAURIE LEIKER

Every day, we're surrounded by buzz words, often used by those who know little of their meaning or intent. Words like "proactive" or "forward-thinking" are thrown out in business communications like they're candy, yet can anyone truly understand the meaning?

"Feedback" is one such word. I've heard managers use it time and again in sentences such as "I appreciate your feedback," when they really hate what the employee has said and would rather fire them. In the end, the word becomes diluted and meaningless.

However, feedback, when done properly, can add inestimable value to a company, its managers and employees, while building the group into a cohesive team, all working to make the company successful and profitable.

So exactly what is "feedback?"

Feedback is two-way communication with a purpose. From a management standpoint, it could be from a manager to employee, employee to manager, between employees but there's always a purpose.

The skill, then, comes in when ensuring the feedback is constructive, not divisive, and YOU are the one who gets to decide.

2 "GOOD" FEEDBACK VS "BAD" FEEDBACK

LAURIE LEIKER

Not all two-way communication is good; we've all been on the receiving end of some pretty bad communication, whether in the home, at school, on the road or at work. But is all negative feedback "bad?" What is the impact of "good" feedback versus "bad" feedback?

Think about when you were a child. How did you feel when your mom said, "I can't believe you only got a B on that paper!" or "Sure, you made your bed, but what about all the clothes on the floor?" Certainly, you felt downtrodden and disheartened, right? No one looks back at communications like that with warm feelings.

Now, think about when your mom said, "Wow! I can't believe you got a B on that paper!" or "Thank you for making your bed, sweetie. Can you help me pick up the clothes? That would be a big help." Better, right?

Both are saying the same thing, but one is an example of "good" feedback, the other "bad." The same holds true in a work setting.

Remember, the goal of being a manager is not just to make sure the work gets done, but to ensure there's a team, all pulling in the same direction. Feedback is just one of the ways in which teams are either built or destroyed.

Good feedback results in:

- Better quality
- Less re-work or re-do
- Faster turnaround of projects
- Less employee frustration
- Better teamwork between all facets of the team
- Closer bonding of employees to the company and those managing.

Conversely, bad feedback:

- Demotivates
- Detaches the receiver from the team
- Detaches the receiver from the company
- Makes the sender feel superior, less connected to the receiver
- Quality and turnaround times suffer
- Team falls apart
- ***Everyone loses***

Remember, that the goal of all workplace communications is to support the company goal, primarily, then the team goal, then the individual goal. In order to make that happen, the manager or team leader needs to ensure that everyone on the team is moving in the same direction, all attached to each other, the team and the company.

So, good feedback will:
- Motivate change
- Build teamwork
- Strengthen attachment of the receiver to the company
- Strengthen attachment of the sender to the team and the company
- Improve quality and turnaround
- ***Everyone wins***

LAURIE LEIKER

3 MOTIVATING KEYS

LAURIE LEIKER

Giving feedback properly is learned, not automatic, so it's important to take steps to ensure the feedback you're giving is appropriate. There are 5 keys to improving your feedback for quick results:

1. **Use positive words**, regardless of whether the feedback is positive or negative. The word "remember" will ensure the person receiving the feedback will remember it; "don't forget" results in forgetting, because the human brain remembers the action word in a sentence. "Always" is another example of a positive word to use instead of "never;" the receiver will only remember the action after the negative or positive.

2. **Lead with praise**. Everyone has an equal mix of good and bad about them, so why not emphasize the positive, not just the negative? Too many times, managers tend to only focus on what the employee is doing wrong and, conversely, employees only focus on what the manager does that drives them crazy. While the situation itself doesn't change, focusing on what everyone does right first will make for a more positive working environment for everyone involved.

3. **Suggest improvement steps instead of simply pointing out errors**. It's all well and good to tell an employee what they've done wrong, but how can they improve or fix what's not right? As a manager, it's always better if an employee comes to you with a problem and a well-reasoned, thought-out solution, isn't it? So why not allow the employee the same courtesy – outline the issue and suggest improvements. Your job is the build the team and each individual member of that team; just because someone drives you crazy doesn't mean they don't have an important role to play.

4. While **emphasizing the correct way to accomplish something**, remember to include how it's been done incorrectly. Praise the effort, correct the means of obtaining the result.

5. **Listen. Listen. Listen**. If the receiver argues, focus on how best to obtain the desired result. It's not about winning and losing; if you get into a true argument, the only loser is the company and you. Listen to EXACTLY what the receiver is saying; it's feedback. Then, instead of trying to address each point, repeat what you heard, so you understand

and the receiver knows you were listening, then ask the receiver to join with you to find a solution. Everyone will always agree to help if you ask them; think about how you feel if someone asks you for help versus tells you what to do – you'll always help.

LAURIE LEIKER

4 WOULD YOU RATHER …?

LAURIE LEIKER

So now, you decide. Here are examples of two different ways of saying the same thing; which would you rather hear?

A: You CANNOT just stop in the middle and leave it for someone else to finish. You MUST finish anything you start; we're not here to pick up your slack. I'm reassigning you the task but you don't have as much time. Just get it done!

B: I know it's a difficult task. How about we work together to figure out an easier way to get it done? (or) How would you suggest we do it better? I don't always know the perfect way to get things done; you probably have a better idea.

A: Great job! I know it's tricky, so let's look at it together to make sure I'm not missing something.

B: I thought I told you to look that up! You're supposed to have the knowledge to get this done. I shouldn't have to tell you how to do it! I'm going to just give it to Jones; he always gets it right.

A: What do you mean you lost the client? How could you argue with him in front of the rest of his team? I don't care how unreasonable he was! You should have just sat there and taken it like a man!

B: It's ok. We can't always keep every client, even though we'd like to. I appreciate how you tried to show the benefits of staying with us and remaining calm, even though he was being unprofessional in his attitude toward you. I can always count on you to be professional.

See how each of the two scenarios play out? In one, you're ensuring the person's dignity remains intact, while at the same time offering a chance for the receiver to figure it out for himself/herself. In the other, your goal is only to hurt the other person. Think about it: If you use poor judgment in your choice of words, you actually are robbing the other person of their dignity, with the end goal only to win the conversation, not to ensure the company goals are met.

5 FINAL THOUGHTS

LAURIE LEIKER

- Remember – your team is only as good and as strong as the feedback you're providing and your ability to focus on the positive. If you're positive, your team will be as well. If your style of communicating is negative, you will suffer poor morale, high employee turnover and poor performance – who wants that?
- You're an employee too. The employees you're mentoring and supervising are where you were not that long ago. Always treat your team members in the same manner you would like to be treated.
- If you're not seeing the best in people, it's up to you to bring the best out by listening, providing positive feedback, finding opportunities to praise the good and build your team.
- Think about how you'd like to be communicated with and what works for you, then apply it to your employees.

- Remember that the person you're talking to is just trying to get it right and do the best they can; no one comes to work and thinks they're going to just make a mess of things all day. Sometimes, trying harder not to make mistakes ends up in bigger mistakes being made. Don't add your frustration on top of someone else's.

ABOUT THE AUTHOR

Laurie Leiker brings 20+ years of communications, training and development to bear on helping managers learn how to bring out the best out of their employees, build their teams and reach corporate goals.

Laurie lives in Austin, Texas, the music capitol of the world, and enjoys speaking to others about being the best they can be.

www.ingramcontent.com/pod-product-compliance
Lightning Source LLC
Chambersburg PA
CBHW071555170526
45166CB00004B/1685